How to Achieve
Digital Immortality

Digital Archiving and
Preservation for Everyone

Tomas Svoboda

Some links in this book contain affiliate codes.

ISBN of the paperback version: 9781796875584

Table of Contents

Why Preserve

There is a Mexican wisdom saying that one dies three times
  • when one learns of their mortality
  • when one's physical body ceases to function
  • when one's name is last spoken
We have little chance of delaying the first two but the third one can be dealt with.

We all would like to be remembered long after we are gone. Digital technology gives us powerful tools to achieve that. However the same digital technology is also very keen in deleting information and creating an overwhelming maze where information gets lost.

This book would like to help you treat your digital assets in ways so as to make them – and your name – survive long into the future.

There is a whole rapidly growing branch of library science which strives to preserve books and other digital content for posterity using very sophisticated, methodical and complicated means. In this book we will try to shield the reader from those complexities and give them simple recipes usable in real life.

Note:

These efforts are not to be confused with the utopian (or rather dystopian) concepts of "Virtual Immortality" or "Digital Immortality" which envision the possibility of transferring a complete human conscience and subconscience to a computer.

What to Preserve

We all have lots of digital assets (and also analog ones waiting for digitization) around us including photos, documents, emails, videos etc. Some of these we see as important and/or interesting, other less so. Now how do we select those pieces that are worthy of being cared for and preserved?

1. **By Description :**
   One handy method will come our way soon: We will see in the next chapters that in order to make a piece of content accessible for posterity we need to describe it thoroughly on many levels. And this logic comes back at us: **If we can provide a good description, dating etc. for a piece of content explaining why it is interesting then this might very well be the piece that deserves preservation.**
   In other words: If we expect someone in the future to spend time consuming our information why not spend some time and effort describing and "*wrapping*" that information for them.

2. **By Subjective Value:**
   The second criterion is a natural one: What it is that you would like to pass on. You are the best expert on your life and work so you may very well know what you want your descendants to see. This does not have to be anything of the usual memorabilia. It can be something completely unusual; just make sure it is understandable **why** this is memorable.

3. **By Data Size:**
   Another not terribly important criterion is the **data size.** Naturally big data objects like video will eat a lot of our resources when it comes to storage. So we might want to prioritize smaller objects like texts or images. However

with the immense storage opportunities we usually have available this factor might easily lose its importance. Most probably it will come into play only when dealing with videos which constitute the largest of our usual data objects.

What NOT to preserve

The digital archive that we are about to create is intended to be distributed and propagated widely. The intent is for it to be easily available for its audience and therefore we will employ no security limitations that would get in the way of that propagation.

Don't get me wrong – we will be concerned about security but our enemy will be loss of information, not unauthorized access.

Count on it that everything you put in the archive will be made public. So **avoid archiving anything potentially embarassing or anything that should remain permanently secret**.

Moreover we can be certain that modern Artifical Intelligence and Data Mining techniques will make it possible to find information even if it is hidden in clutter and unfindable by today's means. Like they say in the Bible: *What you have said in the dark will be heard in the daylight, and what you have whispered in the ear in the inner rooms will be proclaimed from the roofs. (Luke 12:3)*

Who to Preserve for? (Targeting the Unknown Audience)

We are preparing our digital information to be consumed (read, watched, admired etc.) by people in the future who we know very little about. We don' t know what their interests will be or what technology they will have available. While we still want to deliver them our content we must find ways to make sure that

- they find our content
- they find our content interesting
- they can read and understand our content

It is safe to assume that we are preparing the content for some distinct group of people who may be our descendants or the descendants of our work in some way. With such assumption we will find areas of common interest and "*market*" our content to them with a reasonable chance of success.

Another target group would be future historians or "digital archaeologists" who will be searching for digital artifacts while striving to summarize these to paint a broader picture of our times.

We are very much in the dark as to what the future target group will have available in terms of technology. It is possible that technology will continue to evolve rapidly and condemn many of our methods and ways to oblivion. Or vice versa technology may devolve and become scarce which -again- would make it difficult to consume our digital memories. Throughout this book we will strive to package our digital memories in such ways as to make them consumable in the widest possible spectrum of futures.

Why is the Content Important?

The key point here is to communicate to your future audience why the materials you have collected and passed on are important. This may take the form of a written description that you will distribute in various ways for them to notice.

The first step in that direction is making sure and believing yourself that your collection is really important. Such belief will give you added energy to do a good preservation job.

Achieving that realistic conviction will take a lot of research into the topics of your archiving be it family history or any narrower specialty.

Try to put yourself in the shoes of the future readers -what they know and what might be surprising for them. It cannot be wrong to convey your personal touch on events or facts that are widely known. Like

- If you are Alexander Fleming there is little use in declaring "*I invented penicillin*". Much more interesting would be to describe the mistakes, frustrations and dead-ends on the way to the discovery.

- If you have lived through an interesting time like an important election or a disaster etc. it cannot hurt to convey your personal impression of what lead to the result. Like maybe how and why the people around you have voted.

You are the curator

Curators are the educated people who take care of collections in museums and galleries. Their brains are a part of those institutions because they carry in their heads a substantial part of knowledge that fails to be recorded in written documentation.

In case of a small archive like that of a family or a village you will most probably be the single brain holding most of the knowledge and know-how regarding the archive.

Use Your Brainpower and Your Memories

You are probably the only person in the world equipped to navigate and correctly understand the contents of your archive. Use that power and try to insert the maximum of your knowledge into the archive itself.

Example:

You face a roll of film that gives you no clue of when it was shot and why. However you spot one picture of a child with a birthday cake topped by N candles. You use your best judgment as to who the child might have been and when his Nth birthday was. You make your best guess and apply the resulting date to the whole film roll (see Advantage of the Roll on p. 70) believing that it was all shot in similar time.

This is almost detective work and most probably you are the only person in the world capable of doing it. So get to it while you are still alive :-)

Capture and Record as Much Information as Possible

Find all possible creative ways to insert your thoughts and memories into the archive because that is the only way of passing it on to those people in the future.

12

In this chapter we will attempt to list the most common dangers that might lead to the loss of our (*presumably digital*) information. It is obvious that any single one of these factors is enough to complete the destruction so we have to avoid all of them to prevent that fate. Throughout this book we will put together ways of doing that.

Why am I putting this negativistic chapter almost at the beginning of the book? I would say that any preservation effort is a fight against entropy (decay of information) in its many various forms. So I wanted to describe as soon as possible what we are standing against - "know your enemy".

BTW The following list is a much simplified reflection of the part of Library Science that has to do with Long Term Digital Preservation. The teams of professionals at national libraries and archives are dealing with basically the same list though on a much deeper level.

Physical Artifacts Lost or Damaged

In the physical world the artifacts tend to live as only a single instance. It is not very usual or easy to have them replicated. They can be lost, destroyed or damaged in a multitude of ways. This amounts to the single big reason for digitization – which is transforming our precious heritage to a digital form that can be replicated – and therefore protected as multiple instances – extremely easily.

Acidic Paper

One especially troubling case are any prints from the 19th century which may likely be printed on cheap paper containing acids. This kind of paper decays over time and it may soon be gone. The best thing (*outside of expert restoration*) that we mere mortals can do is to make digital copies so that we have at least something left if the original dies.

If we do have anything as old among our treasures: I would recommend ASAP digitization for any paper artifacts from the 19th century regardless of how they appear.

File(s) Unavailable

This subchapter containing several specific situations deals with the most obvious situation when your digital files cease to exist which may happen through several mechanisms. The easy part is that these losses are usually quickly detected. The worst possible scenario is a file is lost quietly without getting noticed for a time so long that backups expire out of relevance.

The countermeasures are obvious: Run a good system of backups.

Deleted File

It happens to everyone that we accidentally erase a file or overwrite it by something wrong. If we have at least some backup in place we can get around this one quite easily. Just be sure that the backup saves several copies back in time so that our mistake does not propagate into the backup as well before we find and correct it.

Lost Access to Cloud

Nowadays we tend to store a lot of our content online "in the cloud" because it is so comfortable to access that content from anywhere as long as the internet exists and works. The access however is guarded massively against unauthorized access and those safeguards can easily turn against us, for example in case of identity theft.

The obvious countermeasure is to keep at least one backup copy in our physical possession e.g. on a hard disk.

Cloud Provider Dead

Beware that the companies that provide our cloud storage and other services usually have no conscience and can stop working any time they like. This has happened with many website providers and led to loss of much valuable content. BTW these mishaps have contributed much to the emergence of web archiving and preservation.

Or the cloud provider may still be alive but has lost some of the users' data. This case is not very different because under these circumstances they are likely to be dead soon anyway.[1]

We should be aware of these possibilities and counter them - again- with a good backup in our physical possession.

Bit(s) Lost in Storage (BitRot)

Now things start to get more interesting. We all know that in digital systems all information is stored in the form of "bits" which take the form of tiny electronic switches whose only two options are to be "*on*" or "*off*" - or "*one*" or "*zero*" as the programmers would prefer to say. These tiny states are often stored in the form of electric charges (as in flash drives and Solid State Disks) or magnetic fields (as in hard drives and magnetic tapes). Here the state -whether the bit is on or off- always depends on whether the charge exceeds some given threshold.

---

1   This sentence was inspired by news on 2019-03-18 that MySpace network has lost 12 years worth of users' historical data.

The physical charges however decay in time so it may happen that a bit changes randomly - even though much effort is dedicated to preventing and delaying this.

A failure of a single bit can cause a perturbation of any unpredictable size - from changing a single letter in a text to making a whole document unreadable or even crashing a whole computer. We can easily imagine that if let this "Bit Rot" go on long enough it will have caused irreparable damage.

So the maxim here is that we act so as not to lose not a single bit of the trillions we own and work with. It can be done with some reasonable care.

Following is a list of storage methods in the order of their resilience to BitRot sorted from worst to best:
- flash drives and memory cards ☹
- individual hard disks
- burned DVDs, CDs and Blu ray disks ☺
- hard disks in RAID (redundant) sets
- special long-lasting DVDs and Blurays(M-Disc)
- disk arrays with consistency controls (disk scrubbing) ☺

One specific method of guarding against BitRot is to compress the files (or whole folders) using some tool that uses checksums to ascertain the integrity of files (e.g. 7ZIP) However that would significantly worsen the accessibility of the archive both now and in the future.

Incomplete Information in Storage

This is a tricky one: Many forms of digital documents depend on pulling some content from other digital objects. This is typical of web (or HTML) pages. These pages -in their own structure- contain text but for images they reach out elsewhere. The page contains a "link" which says where to look for the desired piece of content - for example an image. All is fine as long as the image stays where it is supposed to be. If the image is moved or deleted (or renamed etc.) the page that tries to include it will lose some of its content without being modified itself.

This applies mostly to images, audiovisual content and fonts.

For fonts this problem is almost ubiquitous and mostly ignored: Fonts are usually handled by the operating system, not by the application itself (and usually are not stored with the document) so for example if we open an old Word document we usually get it rendered using different fonts than when it was created. Most of the world ignores this problem though it can lead to distortion of the document.

The underlying reason for these omissions is that certain resources like fonts are omnipresent and widely available at the time of creation of content that we take this as granted and neglect to include them in our digital files.

As a countermeasure we will prioritize such document formats which encapsulate all the content in a common "wrapper" so that all of it travels through space and time together without any partial losses. Examples of such "wrapper" types is an "epub" ebook (if built correctly) or PDF/A where the "A" stands for "archivable".

Obsolete Format

Again as we know anything we store on a computer is a sequence of bits. There are infinite possibilities of how those bits can be arranged to represent some form of our knowledge like a text or an image. These representations are usually called file formats. A file format is a recipe telling the computer which bit means what in order to reconstruct the meaning of the file.

These file formats have developed wildly during the computer era. Basically every programmer who is designing some function may design their own file format for storage. So inevitably we end up with a myriad file formats only some of which are useful in the long run.

And worse than that: Some file formats have been used widely in the past and later slipped into oblivion as computer programs evolved and as software companies came and went. That oblivion means -among other consequences- that tools for accessing those formats are no longer maintained and available. This may leave us in a situation when we have perfectly preserved digital documents from the past and no way of reading them. This is typical of old text processors like maybe WordStar, ChiWriter, WordPerfect ... just to name a few.

Sometimes even the software producers within a single product abandon their own formats in favor of new better ones. CorelDraw users can testify to that being unable to open their files created with early versions of the same product.

The countermeasure is to save our information in well known formats, perhaps even in several formats in parallel and especially to avoid any exotic or custom formats.

Further in this book in the chapter *Various Content Types to Preserve* beginning on page 33 we will discuss the specifics of various file formats for the usual content types.

Missing Context or Language

For understanding some materials we need a preliminary knowledge of other topics. E.g. when discussing the workings of a rocket engine we need to know some basic chemistry in regard to its propellants and need to know a common system of units to understand the temperatures, dimensions etc. So we should take a moment to think what background materials the recipient might need for a good understanding - and to provide these as well.

And we need to know the language used in those materials. While in our time frame we probably will not worry that our language might be forgotten there are cases in human history where documents are available though their language is unknown. In this respect it may be wise to examine whether your materials use any special (scientific perhaps) language that might be unavailable to the recipient.

Let me give some trivial examples: Americans might use the phrase "*Drink the Kool Aid*" without giving it a second thought because "*everybody knows*" that it refers to a mass suicide. However for someone in a different culture this may be a puzzle.

Or in some cultures Friday the 13th is considered a day of bad luck. One might use it in this context without realizing that in a different culture or epoch the meaning might be unclear.

The first step that comes to mind when encountering an unknown concept or a phrase is to look it up on Google. Well, Google as a service might not be available in the future. So let's try Wikipedia. There is a decent chance that the contents of Wikipedia will be preserved longer and better than most other information from our era. So we might use it as a rule of thumb that anything that is explained on Wikipedia will be understandable in the future. And if something is not available on Wikipedia you can insert it yourself.

My Tip:

In order to prevent the aforementioned loss of context be sure to include in your archive even technical information like the types of equipment used to record your data, maybe even its user manuals, perhaps even dictionaries etc.

> *Maybe even a copy of this book could be included in your archive :-) to explain your intentions.*

We may have perfectly preserved digital files but with no reason why someone would take interest in them. This happens easily when context is lost and paths are not provided that would lead a potential reader toward the asset.

Finally there can be perfect digital files full of useful information stored a.k.a. hidden in places that are difficult to find or impossible to identify.

*Data is only effective if it is cleaned, labeled,
curated, understandable and accessible*
- Kirk Borne, Astrophysicist and Principal Data
Scientist at BoozAllen

In front of us is a task of designing a system - an organization - that will enable us to gather, classify and describe our digital assets in the most efficient ways.

The tools we have most readily available are file naming and - in many cases - some metadata which can be connected to those files.

It is our job now to design such a system that will carry the most useful information and self-organize our content as effortlessly as possible.

The Big Picture

Continuous Effort

Preserving your informational heritage is likely to be an ongoing - maybe lifelong - activity, not a one time act. More likely than not it will take time to search out and organize various valuable materials. Even after we have made some significant steps in preservation we will still keep finding new worthy things.

Of course you will not be devoting your full time to digital preservation. Rather you will be revisiting it once in a while in the long run - maybe once or twice per year. Because we might forget a lot between the revisits we should organize our effort in simple and self-explanatory ways so that we do not mess things up due to forgetfulness.

Keep it Together

In professional digital preservation efforts it is very important to separate what is in and what is out *(of the archive)*. What is to be preserved and what is not. The professional digital curators put a lot of work into making sure that everything that is inside is taken care of in a very meticulous way so letting something in is a big scrupulous process. We will not need to be so stringent but some things we do need to keep clear.

One of these is keeping all of our digital valuables together in one space. We might call this space an "**Archive**" on the computer. That way it will be simple to remember that anything we do regarding preservation will be done in this space. Like copying the whole contents onto a medium and storing it somewhere.

We should avoid mixing up the Archive area with our daily work spaces or backups. That means avoiding edits in the Archive. What has entered the Archive *(the pros would say it was* **Ingested***)* is destined to stay there unchanged for eternity, not to be edited anymore.

If there is a really pressing need to change something in the archived files *(like perhaps transforming the files to fit a new technology)* it should always be done on a separate copy while retaining the original also.

The Archive space under our personal circumstances should be a disk space

- on a drive large enough to last for years
- technically stable and reliable
- not internal in a computer - external is better when migrating computers.

We will get to more details in the "Storing..." chapter – on p.47 . However there is no shame starting the archive on any available storage and migrating it later.

Once we have our Archive space staked out we can start doing inside it all that follows.

File System

There are many different ways of storing information in computer systems. There are various databases and other ways of converting meaningful information to the proverbial streams of ones and zeros.

One way has become so widespread that we might even consider it somehow natural - that is the hierarchical file/folder system used in Windows, Mac and almost everywhere where data is exchanged. The system carries well across all sorts of networks, CDs, DVDs and other media.

With this omnipresence it is reasonable to assume that this way of organizing information will somehow find its way into the future and will be readable and understandable for a long time to come. In other words we might expect that someone in the future who tries to read our content and is not a computer scientist will have access to tools letting them readunderstand our folders and files.

However not all flavors of the file/folder system are the same. There are limitations as to the length of names and permissible characters used in the names. Because we can expect our history-making archives to be copied and migrated among various systems we should stick to the "*least common denominator*". It will be wise therefore to limit our names to some reasonable length like 40 characters *(actually the 8.3 -8 characters name plus 3 characters extension -, standard of MS-DOS would be the safest but with too little room for a meaningful description)* and use only the English alphabet (A..Z,a..z) plus numbers (0..9) plus maybe some of the special characters defined a long time ago in MS-DOS:

( ) - _ { }

Specifically we should exclude spaces and dots in our filenames to avoid unnecessary mess.

So let us use the file/folder system to the maximum and hope the our future consumer will feel the same way about it.

No Folderish Content

In Windows and similar operating systems we are used to the fact that a Folder (a.k.a. Directory) is a named entity that has no other function that to contain other files. However in some systems it may be possible to have "Folderish" documents with a meaning/content of their own which can still hold other files. One instance of that approach would the WWW where a page can contain text and still link to its subpages.

For the sake of simplicity let us stick to the Windows way where a Folder is nothing but a named container.

File Names

File names are the most obvious place to enter descriptive information so that it could be easily found. No just found but also sorted. Sorting is probably the most useful power associated with filenames. If we put something meaningful and sortable at the beginning of the name we get the benefits of sorting for free.

So what should the beginning be like? It could be many things like people's names or library codes but in the vast majority of cases it is the date and time associated with the asset - like the date a photo was taken or when an article was written. So from my experience the overwhelming recommendation will be to start file names with a sortable date.

Sortable means that the big units are in front like: **2019-02-14** (This happens to be the international *ISO 8601 standard.)* or

20190214 or similarly. I prefer the first *(standardized)* way because it lets me read the dates easily. However – whatever you choose - the really big task is to remain consistent across all your archive.

If the exact date is not known we can leave just the year or year/month like 2019-02

And please: Always write the day and month numbers as 2 digits - like 2019-03-01, not 2019-3-1. It will help your sorting very much.

So the contents of my archive folder might look like this:

1969_Vladivostok_letter.jpg	2015-1-25 21:51	JPG File	83 KB
1970_SvobodaT_TotinChip.jpg	2012-6-25 18:29	JPG File	222 KB
1989-12-11_italian_fiscal_no.jpg	2018-2-2 20:52	JPG File	128 KB
2003_Krizanov_Tomas_Svoboda_bubn...	2018-7-9 17:11	MP4 Video	56.664 KB
2006-08_SvobodaT_IDcard.pdf	2015-12-17 13:09	PDF File	976 KB
2010_04_dental.jpg	2010-4-14 17:09	JPG File	722 KB
2010_09_dental.jpg	2010-9-9 11:59	JPG File	482 KB
2010_Tomas_opencard_001.pdf	2010-9-2 8:10	PDF File	1.291 KB
2010-VISA.jpg	2012-6-25 18:17	JPG File	134 KB
2011_SvobodaT_tax.pdf	2012-3-26 19:44	PDF File	708 KB
2011_US_withholding.pdf	2012-3-26 19:39	PDF File	248 KB
2012_SvobodaT_passport.txt	2016-11-11 14:01	Text Docu...	1 KB

Even though there are widely different items inside like copies of passports, financial documents and dental X-rays they are all clearly sorted according to the one parameter they have in common which is time.

If we put a date at the beginning of the filename it is good to continue with a name -or something similarly identifiable- right after the date. The sorting will not work there so much but it will be good for easy recognition.

Try to put into the file name as much unique identification as possible - names of people, places and events are the most obvious choices rather than general terms like "meeting" or "excursion" etc.

Imagine that years from now you will be searching for something specific and try to help yourself in advance. Say "1983_Robert_in_Budapest" is better than "meeting_my_uncle".

Folders

Files often have their native names which would be unreasonable to mess with. Like files that make together a web page or the original takes for a movie - if we changed those file names we might break the bigger picture. Or we might like to retain the numbering sequence of photos from a digital camera etc. In these case it makes a lot of sense to keep a set of files together with their intact original names and place them all in a common folder/directory which can be named anything - perhaps according to our date-first standard. Again this will give us a naturally sortable structure while retaining the inherent logic of the files inside.

It is even quite reasonable to set up a date-named folder/directory/container for each and every piece of content even if it should contain only a single file that keeps its original name.

Temporary File Naming

When working on the digitization of some set of materials (*e.g. unpacking the proverbial shoe-box*) we often do not have the information needed to correctly name the items. And it is not important at the moment: At that particular moment it is important to maintain awareness and order of what we are doing and get back to describing it later.

So when I start unpacking another antique box I would probably proceed like this:

- Create a new disk folder/directory (named perhaps box01) to contain all that I will find in there

- Take photo(s) of the contents of the box and put it in the abovementioned directory

- Take out the first item (maybe an envelope on top of the box) and place its photo in its own directory (e.g. *box01/ A_envelope01*)

  - If the contents of the taken-out item is obvious we can mark it in the directory name e.g. "*A_1999-02-02_Niagara_Falls_box01_envelope01*". The initial letter is to help our temporary organization and we will get rid of it later

- Digitize the contents of the item and put it in the same directory

- Repeat with all the items in the box

- Make sure you have covered all the items you intended to

- Return all the items into the box and mark the box as "Digitised/archived on [date] and stored as [file address]"

- Retain a backup copy of the proceeds of your digitisation effort as it stands right now

- Examine the contents of the digitised items, add descriptions and move them to proper places in your archive while getting rid of the temporary „A..B etc." markings

Metadata

This is a rather fancy and progressive way of attaching descriptive and helpful information to data files. Metadata meaning "*above data*" are pieces of information that add some useful context like geolocation, names of people involved, date-time when picture was taken, camera type etc etc. There are even provisions for attaching free form texts like descriptions. This is most mature in digital photos where the metadata recording formats have proliferated and are alive in many mainstream software and hardware system working with the standard JPEG image file standard.

Thus the files become self-describing to some extent.

As seductive as these techniques seem they are far from standardized which means that not all current and future systems will be able to read these and even worse the metadata might get erased/forgotten during a possible migration from one system to another.

If we were an expert team at a national library we would probably have the ambition and capability to see to the preservation of all such metadata but being a humble ordinary person we cannot expect such luxury. So the advice will be to use the metadata richly but make sure that our content makes sense even without them.

If you are new to the concept of Metadata there is one specific exercise I would recommend: Sign in to Wikimedia Commons

commons.wikimedia.org and upload at least one photo while filling in all the requested additional info including location etc. Once you have achieved that you will have become an experienced metadata curator.

commons.wikimedia.org

HTML Guide

There is one elegant technique of attaching descriptive information to a data collection. That would be a HTML (a.k.a. webpage) file at the "root" of your archive. What differentiates HTML over a plain text file is its ability to include links to documents and other pieces of content located not just on the internet but on any filesystem including your desktop and/or archive server.

Manual editing of HTML documents has currently fallen out of fashion but still there are a number of good HTML editing programs available. (google for "HTML editor".) One highly recommendable is the Mozilla Kompozer.

The HTML document will let you enter freeform text (in a future-proof format) to describe what is what in your archive and why is it important.

The Whole Structure

Apart from correctly naming your files and directories and keeping them tidy you will need to give some meaningful shape to your whole archive. While there is no single best way here on the right is one example that works for many people:

You can see here that the archive from its top level is divided into topics of

- Cars

- Videos

- Houses

- People

- Photos

- Products

These are some of the possible groupings that will make your content intuitively organized.

Put it in Context

You will certainly be putting in lots of different information about your life and work etc. That is fine. However you may want to enhance the story of your life by including some "neighborhood" - some of the factors that have formed you like your favorite books, movies, maps and

Archive
  Cars
    Mustang
      1998_Purchase
      2005_Sale
      Insurance
      Photos
    Sierrra
    VW
  Family_videos
    1960--1979
    1980--1999
    2000--2009
    2010--2019
  Houses
    Houston
    Vienna
  People
    John
    Mary
      flying
      jobs
      medical
      schools
  Photos
  Products

such. Simply anything that may help the future reader understand how you came to be what you are.

Workflow

This is an extremely important takeaway:

As you will be working with different versions of your files, shifting them around and periodically forgetting what you did last time:

> *Be sure to have your sequence of actions (a.k.a. Workflow) well thought out and planned in advance.*

> *And try to save your files in an orderly meaningful scheme and do not save any files that do not have a clear purpose. There is nothing worse in this effort than combing through multiple similar versions of the same content and contemplating which of these versions was meant to contain the most useful information.*

Avoid Confusion

While maintaining multiple copies of your data for backup be sure to have a single (clearly distinguished) master copy where you make the changes and additions that later propagate to the backups.

Making changes to multiple copies and trying to consolidate them later is a path to hellish confusion and to losing faith in your preservation project.

The task here to find ways for storing various types of content so that they could be read as far as possible into the future.

This has a lot to do with file formats. Generally we will be trying to find formats which

- are very widespread giving hope that even sometime in the future they will be remembered and understood and/or

- are well documented so that the tools for reading them could be reconstructed in the future.

To get ahead of myself: In most cases the result of our search will lead us to a double way of storage where

- one format is more future-proof but somehow limiting

- another format captures more quality from the original but may be less understandable in the future

My recommendation will be to store in both formats in parallel.

Mixing Formats

Our digital information comes in various kinds and formats all of which may relate to the same event or topic. It makes a perfect sense to put all related files inside the same folder to explicate their relationship.

E.g. a folder called "2019-07_African_safari" would contain photos, videos and maybe even diary texts of the same series of events. It is much better than the bad old way of organizing folders by content type e.g. "photos, spreadsheets, documents, audio...

Preserving Photographs

Photos are arguably the most important and widespread digital asset calling for preservation. The explosive growth of digital photography over the last two decades has flooded our world with trillions of images which sit on desktop computers and notebooks waiting to be erased by the next system crash.

The prevalence of digital photos is so great that there are many digital preservation efforts that deal with photographs only. We should accept it as a fact that photos are likely to constitute the bulk of your digital archive.

Image formats

There are lots of file formats used for storing images. We will list some of the more important ones and conclude how to use them in archiving of photos.

JPEG

Stands for "Joint Photography Experts Group" and is alternately abbreviated as JPEG or JPG.

Most of the photos from consumer grade digital cameras comes in this format. Even if you ignored everything except JPEG you would probably still preserve a lot.

The proliferation of digital photography has brought a very strong standard: The JPEG file format has become so widespread that it has a huge hope of being recognized long into the future. This is of utmost importance for our intention of keeping our photos usable for the future.

The main disadvantage of the JPG format is that it describes each color channel (*out of Red, Green, Blue*) by an 8 bit number - giving only 256 possible values. In some sensitive images (e.g. soft foggy tones) this can lead to spoiling the impression.

However for a huge majority of photographic situations the 8 bit depth is sufficient.

JPEG files are produced not only by digital cameras but also by most scanners which makes the format even more important.

*I will now get ahead of myself by recommending that **we always save a JPEG version of a photo** alongside any other format we may be storing.*

JPEG2000

This is an advancement above and beyond the limitations of the original JPEG. It allows a bigger bit depth (= dynamic range) and lots of new features. Unfortunately it has not yet achieved a widespread recognition so we cannot fully rely on it for the future.

RAW

This is not a single format, rather an abbreviation for various custom formats where different camera makers store image data in their most native form. Obviously these RAW files carry the most original information so it makes sense to store them alongside their JPEG derivatives. The danger here is that these files will become unreadable as camera makers shift to new types and new ways of encoding their images.

TIFF (Tagged Image File Format)

This is another mature image format used typically in high quality scanning. It has a higher bit depth as well as capability to store multiple images/pages. It is thoroughly standardized and widespread among professionals. Storing TIFFs probably is future-proof when seen by libraries and museums; the question is whether the future non-professional whom we are targeting will have the correct tools available to read TIFFs..

MPO (Multi Picture Object) for 3D

This is a simple extension of the JPEG enabling to encapsulate several JPEG images in a single file. Typical it is used for stereoscopic photography to keep the left and right eye views together. Though internally it is very similar to JPEG it is not widely recognized and may not be readable in the future.

I do use this format produced by my rare 3D camera but always keep one of the pair of photos aside as JPEG. If someday mankind will really embrace 3D photography then my pictures will be useful. If not the ordinary JPEGs will still do the job.

EXIF Metadata

This widely used feature serves for adding various metadata to image (JPEG or TIFF) files. It enables a lot of informational enrichment like geotagging, marking equipment used, author, exposure and especially names and descriptions.

The big advantage here is that the metadata is directly embedded in the image file so it will stay there as long as bit-level preservation is maintained. However EXIF is not recognized by all software so there is a risk of it getting lost in conversions or reformatting. Therefore I wholeheartedly recommend to use EXIF intensively but not to rely on it as a single way of describing photos.

Preserving Videos

With video formats it is difficult to forecast which one may be the most future-proof. There are multiple file formats which differ not only in the ways how they directly store the video and audio tracks but also in how they "wrap" a.k.a. organize their content in terms of synchronizing multiple tracks, providing additional information etc. Some are optimized for real time streaming, other for storage. Among these it is really difficult to predict which will be available in the future.

One clue that we might cling to is the immense number of playable (*meaning playable in a standalone player other than computer*) DVDs in existence. Due to being so many of them one might expect that far into the future there will be capabilities (*at least in specialist hands*) to read these - and the same may soon apply to the more advanced BluRay disks. Therefore it seems wise to select a playable DVD as a robust long lasting storage. We can select one of the simpler writable variants (e.g. DVD-R), couple it with a long lasting media and we have a reasonable hope for longevity. However the MPEG2 derivative compression used here is a lossy one (as opposed to lossless) so it will not store the full 100% quality of your original. To that end I would recommend storing the original in parallel in MP4 format or similar which is lossless though may be less future-proof.

So the optimum solution would be to archive the videos in MP4 format and also burn them onto playable DVDs (or BluRays) **using a program like the "Windows DVD Maker" or *"BurnAware Free"*.**

Of course we would use the long lasting M-Disc media in their DVD-R and BD-R versions respectively.

Converting Between DVDs and MP4

Converting among modern video formats (like MP4, MP2, MKV, WMV, AVI...) is quite straightforward because they all contain more or less the same types of information just encoded in different ways - so it is only a question of some sophisticated number-crunching to convert among them.

With DVDs it gets more difficult because they contain a lot of extra stuff like menus and subtitles which are encoded in a rather primitive way as images (!). This was to satisfy the mass market of players with weak processing power in the 1990's and we still have to live with that heritage.

The effect is that some key information like names of chapters a.k.a. video files are not easily available on the DVD and often have to be typed in manually during the conversion process.

Therefore when organizing our video archive it is much better to maintain the MP4s as the "originals" and create the DVDs as a copy thereof (rather that vice versa).

The conversion from video to DVD can be done easily by multiple free "DVD-burning" programs. *Personally I am content using a program called "Windows DVD Maker"*

In case we really do need to convert from a DVD to MP4 I would recommend an excellent piece of software named "Handbrake" (*I have no idea why the name*). And be sure to check and repair the resulting filenames.

Video sizes

Modern programs and protocols offer us a wide array of options and tradeoffs when it comes to video quality and file size. Basically maintaining a better quality (that goes with bigger resolution) comes with a cost in terms of file size. A larger file size is a burden for all our preservation activities. So the goal is to find the sweet spot where all the visual quality of the original stays preserved and not more. This can be the topic of endless discussions, however I would propose the following (very approximate) rule of thumb which applies to the MPEG-2 format (as used in playable DVDs):

	GB per hour	Hours per DVD (4,5 GB)
Super-VHS, Hi-8 16mm film	2	2
VHS Super8 film	1	4
VHS Long Play Normal8 film	0,7	6

The more advanced MPEG-4 format tends to be 4-5 times more efficient thus producing smaller files as per that ratio.

However:

The previous applies to copies intended for archiving. When it comes to copies for further processing (e.g. visual effects, corrections, etc.) we should always aim for the maximum quality and resolution available.

Text documents have been the first kind of information in the world of computers. It still is the simplest (and probably most future-proof) way of sharing information.

Ever through the computer age there came and went various non-standard formats of storing text which included advanced formatting and markup and made the files less clear to understand without the proper custom software with which it was created. Therefore already today we have trouble reading ancient (*read 20 years old*) files written by the likes of WordPerfect, ChiWriter, WordStar etc. So this raises a big question of how to format and store texts to avoid that same fate. Perhaps the best start in that direction is the clean TXT format such as the one produced by Windows Notepad handy editor. Historically this has been the most trivial format storing text in a form most intimately connected to the operating systems of the computers. That simple format was also embedded to transmit the first e-mail messages. Nowadays the TXT format is not as absolutely simple as it used to be - due to the introduction of Unicode symbols for non-English languages - but still it is the simplest environment that the digital world has to offer. So I would always opt for TXT to keep my information ready for future history.

If we absolutely positively need to include formatting not possible with pure TXT then a reasonable second step would be to use a HTML (or X-HTML better still) format. The advantage here is that the formatting is added on top of plain text which remains readable even in lack of proper displaying tools.

On the other side - from the worst: One of the big menaces for keeping a clear maintainable text is Microsoft's DOC format. Certainly it is a good idea to stay away from DOC (older MS Word) format as far as possible. That format is a cryptic mess inside and has caused too many nightmares already. One of its worst problems is its maze of formatting tags (the invisible markers telling how should the text be displayed or printed) which tend to persist even after export to another format. If you do have an important document in DOC the surest way is to export it to pure TXT (no formatting) and work with it from there.

DOCX (newer MS Word) is better (open and better documented) but still not clear enough.

Another important player is the PDF (Print Definition Format), namely the PDF/A variant destined for archiving. Its power is that it captures the faithful image of a printed page while still including the (simple alike TXT) "text layer".

My best idea is to store your documents as PDF/A (produced by many widespread applications like the LibreOffice) with a parallel copy in pure TXT.

We may have some memorable audio recordings in our collection. Historically these used to be the voices of people deliberately recorded for posterity or some musical performances. Since the 1980's however these were replaced by the omnipresent videos. Another archivable category would be your favorite pieces of music which you would like to preserve as important parts of your life story.

Here the simplest format seems to be uncompressed WAV.

There is also the opportunity of storing playable CDs (advantages similar to playable DVDs for video). A small obstacle is that no long-lasting M-Discs are available in the CD variant. The closest thing to longevity would be various gold covered (as opposed to the common aluminum) CD-R media like the following one:

https://amzn.to/2EgiN4c

And: When burning playable CDs be sure to include informational titles for each track/file. The CD format enables this metadata feature much better than the -otherwise more advanced- later DVD format.

The way to include metadata on a playable CD is to use a feature called CD-TEXT supported in better burning programs, like "*BurnAware Free*". This feature enables to fill in the name of the "track" and the author plus other data items including a freeform "Message". These pieces of text can include a lot of useful information that you wish to convey to the users.

If the audio is an original music recording (*including maybe something as trivial as your kids singing at Christmas*) then it would make sense to register its unique ISRC (International Standard Recording Code) number. Registering this means that the recording is included in a central database which is likely to survive long into the future just like the ISBN for books. This will help to keep the recording remembered and getting found in the future. The ISRC code can also be included in the CD-TEXT metadata.

Preserving Websites

Websites either your own or other are an important part of your digital environment. Therefore it is worth the effort to archive some of the important ones.

If it is your own website that you want to archive and you have access to the webserver's file structure then the task is simply to copy the relevant directories.

If you intend to archive a foreign website then it gets a little more complex:

If you need to archive just one or a small number of web pages then you can do this in most web browsers using the function "Save Page as HTML" or similar (unless you have direct access to the webserver's file structure of course). Beware that this will usually output multiple files so be sure to isolate them in a dedicated directory.

When it comes to archiving websites other than your own the good news is that "web.archive.org" may be already doing that for you (we will discuss more about it in the Preservation through Distribution/Online Copies chapter on page 93).

If you need to archive a whole complex foreign website or a bunch of sites you should use a specialized crawling tool to do it.

Preserving Email

Email is a tricky type of content: It is totally self-documenting because every message sent or received contains a wealth of metadata including the "From" and "To" fields, Date etc. Even its body contains text which begs for automatic indexing and searching. However it escapes most file/directory oriented archiving schemes because it tends to live in its own structures not easily convertible to files and directories. Yes, you can convert every single email to a file while retaining most of its content but except for very special important items this would not be worthless effort and empty clutter as most emails we receive are ephemeral or even senseless.

As such your email history lends itself more to Long Term Backup than to real Archiving. And I would propose to treat it as such:

Develop a habit of keeping a backup of all your email history and storing it in your Long Term Backup - you may find it useful when searching for a specific email to or from a specific person years ago.

However some very special email messages that relate to important events in your life do deserve to be archived for the future: In that case use the "Save As" or "Export" function in your email program and convert the email to a TXT or HTML or other format depending on what level of formatting you intend to preserve.

As for myself:
I have my emails since 1996 stored in Long Term Backup.
The total is a 6 digit number. I do occasionally use that
storage to find something of interest but only 2 of those
emails have yet made it to my Archive.

Preserving Various Other Content Types

There are many different content types that we regularly work with but cannot be archived very simply.

Spreadsheets, Presentations

These are highly structured forms of text, multimedia and other content that need the original producing software to duplicate their full functionality. My best guess at archiving these would be to export and archive them as PDF/A along with good descriptions internal (inside the document itself) or external.

Facebook and Similar

There is a lot of enthusiasm for preserving the online life on our social networks. There are tools for storing some parts of one's virtual neighborhood but these do not exceed the requirements of a Long Term Backup. The internal structure of those conversations is so complicated that these can hardly be considered for archiving without substantial manual curation. My best idea would be to export text documents of selected content like "My favorite Facebook posts on Relativity" or "My ICQ conversations with XYZ" and archive those.

Facebook lately has been offering the option of downloading all your content in HTML or XML format. That may be useful but beware of archiving a complicated uncurated nondescript maze of various data.

In this chapter we will discuss how to store our data so that every single bit of information is preserved in exactly the same way it was recorded for as long as possible.

We will need to split this into these areas:

1. Backups - just for ourselves so that we do not lose anything

2. Working Archive Storage - medium term - this is where we will gather and keep our preservables in the course of years, maybe decades

3. Long Term Storage - where our digital heritage will be stored for(almost)ever.

Backups

Backup laws:
- *If you have one copy, you have none.*
- *If you have two copies, and they are on the same place, you have none.*

Let us begin by pronouncing the obvious: Backup is not archiving.
Backups serve only for ourselves that we do not lose the results of our recent everyday work.

And remember: Also our ongoing work in the preservation archive ***should definitely be backed up regularly****. It would be a shame to lose our digital treasure trove before the future has even started.*

Another way of wording the initial theme is the famous 3-2-1 law:

3: Maintain at least 3 copies of your content at all times

2: Have your backups on at least 2 different types of media

1: At least one of your copies has to be off-site

Daily Backups

A good daily (or more often etc.) backup is great for regaining something we lost recently as long as we know what we are looking for. However (given the usual disorder and lack of description) in our digital living spaces it is by far inadequate to be read by someone in the future who does not have our knowledge of the context.

So: Yes let us do backups most efficiently to protect ourselves from losing pieces of our digital world but let us also work on real archiving of our most valuable digital content.

Perhaps the most crucial notion to keep in mind: When designing our backup strategy it is important that some of the backup copies be located off your main site to deal with a fire or similar mishap. The same applies not only to our daily backups but also to copies of our archive.

Long Term Backups

I find it useful to have something between a backup and a real archive for me to easily find some file that I had worked on years ago and did not go through the trouble of archiving it. I call this the Long Term Backup.

It works like this: Whenever I move to a new computer (or cloud storage or a webserver etc.) I copy everything I have on that old system to my storage server. I do not worry that most of the content there is garbage that I will never access as long as it might help me find that single valuable file that would otherwise be lost. With storage prices dropping most of the time the size of the backups is not an issue except for some large objects e.g. movies.

1990-a-dal-ze-zalohy-1998-STARY.DSK	2014-10-28 2:17	File folder
1991-Softwarove-noviny	2018-3-24 18:38	File folder
1997_historicke dokumenty_ze zalohy_...	2014-10-28 2:17	File folder
1998_Infima_PacBell	2014-10-28 2:24	File folder
1998-04-14	2014-10-28 2:18	File folder
1998-11	2014-10-28 2:22	File folder
1999_konec	2014-10-28 2:24	File folder
2000_11_28_NovellInfima	2014-10-28 2:26	File folder
2001_06	2014-10-28 2:27	File folder
2001_ze_zaloh	2014-10-28 2:28	File folder
2002_04_05	2014-10-28 2:30	File folder
2002_x	2014-10-28 2:32	File folder
2003_08_26	2014-10-28 2:33	File folder
2004	2014-10-28 2:37	File folder
2004_INFIMA_Distribuce	2014-10-28 2:46	File folder
2004-03-16	2014-10-28 2:45	File folder
2005_CommTact	2014-10-28 2:46	File folder
2006_WebServer	2014-10-28 2:48	File folder
2007_09_Notebook_CNS	2014-10-28 4:13	File folder

So my historical storage looks like this (forgive some Czech descriptions):

Each of the listed folders contains a whole structure of my working files as it was at that respective time. I am proud to say that I have kept these Long Term Backups since 1990 and have used them quite often to access pieces of my personal history.

If you happen to be important enough for someone to dig in your digital heritage (a.k.a. Digital Archaeology) your Long Term Backup may give them some excellent material. *This is something you may or may not want* :-)

One more remark: The Long Term Backup should be a simple exact copy of the data from your computer - not the custom output of some fancy backup software. Remember that you may not have that software available a few years from now.

And needless to say: This collection we call "Long Term Backup" is a valuable asset itself so it should be backed up as well – meaning that it should exist in at least 3 independent copies some of them being offline.

Working Archival Storage (Medium Term)

In this chapter we will discuss the task of providing dependable storage to our archive for the duration of our lifetime while we still can access it and work on it (and while electricity is being supplied).

This storage solution should fulfill these requirements:

1. Maintain the integrity of our data e.g. protect against BitRot – that means protecting against subtle innocuous data errors (*This prioritizes various error correcting mechanisms.*)

2. Be portable so that it does not have to be recreated when switching computers (This prioritizes external disk boxes.)

3. Protect against big errors e.g. a failure of an entire hard disk. Surprisingly this is not terribly critical because these failures are obvious and if we have a good backup system we will reverse the situation in a straightforward manner. (*However we still want to avoid these failures so this gives priority to robust RAID systems*).

4. Be as simple as possible (to enhance its dependability) In an ideal case the storage system should be as simple as an electrical appliance.

5. Be economical: This will lead us to utilize optimum disk sizes and hibernation to save power when not in use.

This storage should be reliable and stable enough to last at least a few decades without a major disruption. No computer hardware is to be expected to last that long so we must count on migrating the hardware every few years while maintaining every bit of the archived content.

Here I would recommend to use an **external disk or array of disks**. Not an internal disk inside a computer because we want the storage to live longer than a typical computer so we will be connecting it to different computers as time goes.

> *One specific manifestation of the inherent simplicity of this approach goes like this: I used to tell my family "If I die you can just take this box and connect it anywhere like a USB flash drive to access its contents. "*
> *Regardless of the fact that I have it rigged in a rather complicated server setup.*

(This held while I was using a simple hardware RAID box. Not any more now.)

For the sake of avoiding failures of whole disks it would be great to do this on a RAID array. RAID (*Redundant Arrays of Inexpensive Disks*) means that the data is spread across several disks to protect against the failure of any one of them. If one of the disk fails it gets replaced and the whole repairs itself automatically.

By RAID I mean a level of at least 5 on the scale of RAID types. Level 6 would be even better since it protects against 2 failures at once.

> *Yes I am quite picky about the configurations and RAID levels so regardless of my rigorous opinion bear in mind that even the plainest RAID level 1 (just a pair of mirrored disks) is better than no RAID.*

One possibility is to go with a simple hardware-based RAID without too much added functionality. (*Hardware-based means that its functionality is contained in its integrated circuitry rather than in the software of a specialized embedded computer leading to more stability and simplicity.)*

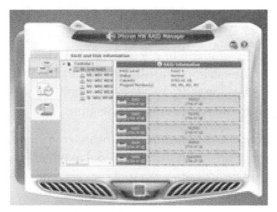

Many hardware RAID appliances are based on reliable JMicron (393/394) chips and can be recognized by variations of this unusually looking management software window.

There is a plethora of reasonable RAID5 arrays on the market.

One great example of a simple hardware RAID: the Sharkoon brand pictured with an appropriate harddisk.

These simple RAID boxes are wonderful tools but we will soon see that they lack some functionality that we may require.

Some of the additional functionalities useful for extended preservation are

- Automatic checking of integrity of fileslies , sometimes called Disk Scrubbing

- Hibernation of disks to reduce power consumption and extend their longevity

As for the Disk Scrubbing please bear in mind that we will be dealing with trillions or quadrillions (in the American sense meaning 10^{12} to 10^{15}) of bits over a period of decades. Under such circumstances it is realistic or even unavoidable to encounter random bit errors which threaten or digital treasures.

As for the power consumption: We intend to have the disks serving us for 5-10 years each and during that time they will consume a value of power on the order equivalent to their purchase price. So it makes sense to turn them off when not in use.

The previous requirements are not easily achievable by simple RAID boxes. So we may have to sacrifice some simplicity to get the job done. That brings us to the category of NAS (Network Attached Storage) Which are basically specialized computers (usually running some flavor of the Linux operating system) that provide the RAID functionality and more.

Capacity

Let us bear in mind that our archive might easily grow to terabytes (if we include videos) and such mass of data is not easy to work with. Just copying the archive from one drive to another may take a week or more so we would want the storage to be as permanent as possible.

If we decide to use the same storage for other purposes like storing commercial movies or backups of PCs (which are reasonable reuses of the investment) we will soon be in the range of terabytes or more. So it is safe to say that we will be assembling our storage as an array of multi-terabyte disks.

From the viewpoint of the cost per terabyte currently the best option are 4 TeraByte disks and that privilege may soon shift to 6 TeraBytes. This is one clue for selecting our disks. We might well begin with a RAID1 pair of 2 disks (just a mirror) of 4TeraBytes and gradually grow to 3 and more disks and reach a capacity of 10+ TB. It will be an advantage if we can support that gradual growth with one NAS box.

> *My personal selection is this:*
> *I have opted for a Synology (~~which is~~ one of the major NAS brands) which supports all my required functions and does so through a simple not-too-technical user interface. My choice was the 5-disk DS1019+ product.*

My DS1019+ NAS array with 5 disk bays

The minimum I would recommend for the serious user is 4 drive bays on DS420j .

If you too opt for a Synology box (or similar) then remember to turn on Disc Scrubbing and Hibernation.

Long Term Storage

Now comes the hard part: How can we store our content so that it would last for decades, possibly centuries without anyone's intervention:

The bad ways:

First of all let us rule out all forms of flash drives and SSDs (*Solid State Disks*) that use an electrical charge to store information. Their retention is limited to several years at maximum. To increase their retention time they may be equipped with mechanism for self-checking and error correction which unfortunately will work only when power is supplied to the device. That we cannot guarantee over a long period of time e.g. when the medium is resting for decades in a box in the basement somewhere.

Then come the magnetic media including hard disk drives. These are more resilient and will hold their content for a decade or more. However the magnetic marks still do dissipate so a good practice would be to copy the content to a new disk location every year or so (hopefully with error checking in place) to make sure that the magnetic records remain fresh. (*Good RAID arrays will do this for us but only as long as we keep them powered and replace their failed disks every few years.*)

So magnetic disk drives go a long way but still are not a means of storage that we could leave unattended for decades.

The practical way: Optical Disks

Optical disks in the mainstream status quo are the omnipresent recordable CDs, DVDs and BluRay disks. The recording takes place by a narrow laser beam burning holes in a thin layer of metal on top of polymer material. The difference between a hole and no hole is the difference between a binary "1" and "0". However in these traditional media the polymer layer tends to degrade over time leading to a lifetime on the order of decades. The standard according to which these media are recorded includes some self-correcting provisions which increase the resiliency and usable lifetime of recordings but still only on the order of decades.

A breakthrough came about 10 years ago when some innovative producers replaced the polymer layer with a much more durable one of metal oxides (*so called "stone disks"*). According to measurements in accelerated aging environments these media are expected to hold their content for at least 200 years and probably even 1000. Recently the technology has matured and is available on the market under the "M-Disc" brand. Like the one in the picture:

amzn.to/2XqOQXS

As additional feature I always opt for inkjet-printable variant of the disks for obvious marking that may save the records from the garbage dump.

These disks of tremendous longevity still can be written and read by many mainstream devices which makes them the obvious way to go for the amateur archivist. I would imply that the M-Discs are currently the single best medium for long term archival available to a non-expert.

M-Disc media come in DVD and BD (Bluray) capacities whose longevity is approximately equivalent. It might be slightly better for the DVDs due to their lesser information density.

One added advantage of optical discs is their low price due to which it is feasible to produce multiple copies in order to distribute the archive widely (as per „Preservation through Distribution" 91)

Currently the capacity of optical disks is limited to 100GB (BD-XL variant) which usually means that our collection will need to be split across several disks.

Lack of devices

Unfortunately not all DVD and Bluray drives can write the M-Disc media. So it takes some searching to set up a good working system.

My favorite among the few is the ASUS BW-16D1HT Bluray drive which has served me well so far. It is full height so it may not fit all enclosures. On the other hand it is a solid construction and good performer.

More Is To Come

While at the time of writing this book the optical discs are the best long term storage solution available to consumers like you and me there may be new developments about to happen:

Among these it seems that technologies for storing information in laser generated dot patterns inside a body of glass may be quite promising in the near future. Microsoft's „Project Silica" may be leading the way in this direction.

Anyway if a new long term storage technology becomes available we will use it happily while all the advice given in the rest of this book will still apply.

What to do exactly

In this chapter we have elaborated on how to best preserve our data. Let us now summarize the steps:

- Keep the master copy of your archive on a RAID/NAS array for as long as you can.

- Keep several backups of the archive locally, remotely and/or in the cloud.

- Make preservation copies on M-Discs and put them in places where they will be eventually found. (We will discuss those placements later in this book.)

So far we have assumed that we have all our material in digital form. Of course that is not always the case. Often we need to convert analog material to digital in order to make it immortal. There are lots of books and instruction out there about digitization; I will not try to duplicate those. Rather I will try to provide simple recipes with the goal of digital preservation in mind.

Important Tip

One of the most basic and simple rules of digitization is this: When you have successfully digitized any material be sure to mark the original clearly to prevent a duplicate digitization of the same material and the chaos that it can cause.

Let us now go through various analog media and see how to digitize them for the future.

Digitizing Photographs

Most often photographs will be the bulk of our digitization efforts due to their richness of information and easy digitization.

Our old photographs are usually found in shoe-boxes full of prints, framed slides or negatives. The process of digitizing these brings along one much useful side effect - giving the collection some structure.

When digitizing we should always resort to the most original form which means prioritizing negatives (or framed slides) over prints. This is simply because the original will always contain more information than subsequent copies (*law of information entropy*) except possibly if the original has significantly degraded over time.

Framed Slides

Many of our valued photos will come in the form of mounted slides. We can find these in many forms some of which will fit in the scanning apparatus and some will not.

The good ones include most paper frames and thin plastic ones. Generally those frames that were applied automatically in developing machines will be OK.

One special type that will not work are double glass mounts. Not only that these are too thick to fit in many rigs but also the glass will tend to produce unwanted interference patterns.

Whenever I encounter a glass mount I take it apart and carefully put the film in a more practical type of mount. There is a lot to pick from in the market but let me introduce my personal favorite found after as much as 40 years of searching:

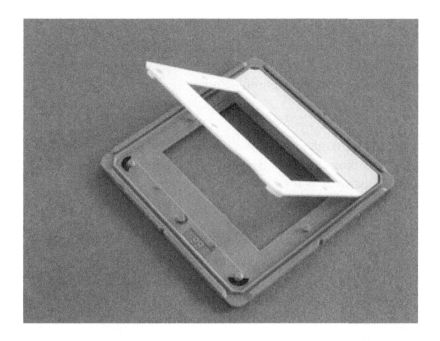

This type called "Reflecta CS Slide Mount" has become my favorite. Its advantages are that it remains in one piece and clicks into place very easily and exactly even when inserting a warped film. It is widely available since probably I am not the only one who likes it.

DIY vs. Commercial

There are lots of commercial services who can digitize your negatives and slides to excellent quality. On the other hand you can just as well decide to do this yourself.

If you opt for a commercial service be sure to check their reputation because you will be trusting them with your irreplaceable materials. Also it would be wise to initially test them on a partial sample not just to test the quality of their output but also to make sure that their digital files will fit in your chosen archiving organization.

Choosing the DIY approach has the advantage of using your apriori knowledge of the material. You -unlike a commercial provider- can easily judge the content of materials, who is who and where does which photo belong.

Scanning Equipment ?

I would love to give you now a sophisticated guide for selecting your scanning equipment: Basically we should be looking for something with

- resolution of at least 2500 DPI (this corresponds to the fine grain of a classical film)
- dynamic range - Dmax like 3.5 or more (this is the range between whitest white and darkest black)
- capacity to process at least 10 images (of 35mm film or slides) in unattended batch
- scan not only 35mm film but also rare formats like 60mm or Instamatic
- longevity of at least 10 thousand scans
- reliability
- usable software and documentation

However after much market watching I found out that (as of now - 2019) for a non-professional who wants a good quality for a reasonable price (let's say below 1000 $ or EUR) there are not many options. The market has been much richer just 10 years ago but let us focus on today: Actually recently I found just one reasonable option:

Epson V800/V850

This excellent scanner has been around since 2006 without substantial changes. At first there were two variants: V700 and V750 which differed only in the number of enclosed film holders. The V700 had one set while V750 had two sets . The double set of holders is actually very handy for the scanning workflow because you can empty and fill one holder while the other one is being scanned. *I had initially purchased V700 but as time went I* *had to buy the second set anyway so next time I would opt for the *50 variant.*

In 2014 the scanner has been upgraded to V800 and V850 types. As far as I understand there were no major functional changes (*well - perfection does not need improving*), just the

- light source was upgraded from incandescent to LED and

- film holders have evolved

so it really remains the same product.

https://amzn.to/2XygP8m

Its qualities have been compared with really expensive professional scanners and the differences were found to be subtle.

The scanner comes with a company software "Epson Scan" which looks old and is far from perfect but lets you set up a decent workflow. Also a more professional "SilverFast" scanning software comes bundled.

....

Those with enough cash might opt for its larger brother the

Epson Expression 12000XL-PH which boasts a double (A3) scanning area and therefore takes in twice the batch of original compared to V800. I have worked with it and found its functionality exactly the same as V700 with better productivity.

https://amzn.to/2BVahY0

The excellent scanner (V700) has served me perfectly for the last 14 years and is the choice for scanning of negatives, framed slides, prints and paper documents.

However there some exceptions where different equipment is useful. One of these is:

35mm (and other) Film Rolls:

Film rolls may be the best quality material in your collection because they are the "originals" from which prints were made. The best possible situation is if the rolls were cut into strips of 6 (or 4) images and stored flat – those are immediately ready for digitization in a flat scanner like the aforementioned Epson V800. However if your films have been stored in rolls (and stayed in that shape for decades you may have to devote some effort to the process of straightening them. Do not try to roll the film in the opposite direction – that would inevitably lead to scratches. Rather it is effective to cut the film, insert the stripes in protective sheets (*some struggle required*) and press the sheets (in a large book etc.) to flatten them.

I have successfully flattened film rolls up to 60 years old but it required months or even years of pressing. So start on it ASAP.

PrimeFilm XA – scanning whole rolls

If your shoe-box contains many 35mm films (usually negatives) in their original form which is a roll of 36 images you may want to ease your workload by scanning them all in a single pass.

There used to be several scanners in the market capable of processing a whole 35mm roll but most have been discontinued. So again there is not much to pick from:

For this purpose I have found one fitting product under a dual identity: In the U.S. it is called <u>Pacific Image PrimeFilm Xas</u>

<u>https://amzn.to/2NtaOVH</u>

while in Europe the same or a very similar scanner is known as Reflecta RPS-10M

To be honest it took some effort to make the scanner work (I used the European version) but it was worth it. The productivity of scanning a whole roll in one batch is a great advantage. The bundled CyberView software is far from perfect - actually the version from the enclosed CD was almost unusable. The key to success was to download an upgrade from the www.scanace.com website.

Advantage of the Roll (or Envelope)

Not just is it easy to scan a whole roll at once, moreover it is inevitable that if a set of images is found on a single roll (whole or cut & enveloped neatly from a lab) those images have to belong together. This is an invaluable clue in comparison with individual prints or framed slides which may have been mixed in unaccountable ways.

Photo Prints

We will certainly come across some photographs where only the paper print is available because its negative was lost (or it is a Polaroid etc.) These will present some of their specific challenges:

Capturing the back side context

Paper prints often have notes written on their back sides which may contain invaluable metadata information. If this is the case I would scan the back side as well as the front and save the file in a way that makes it clear that the two belong together.

The same may apply to envelopes, boxes, bags etc. which have contained our photographic treasures. And also to inscriptions on old slide frames.

Equipment

On one hand the technology required to well scan a print is nondemanding - just about any office scanner will do with the usual resolution of 300DPI

However the manual workflow tends to get quite tedious since you have to insert each photo separately and guide the scanning and post-processing in real time - without much chance for batch processing. Therefore when limited to using a flatbed scanner I am always picky about selecting only the really valuable prints for digitization.

If we have a large enough number of paper photos to justify another investment (200-1000 prints) we may go for a specialized scanner with an automatic feeder. With some limitations any autofeeding document scanner will do (*especially if we can find a duplex one – meaning that it scans both sides of the paper at once*) but there is one piece of hardware that has recently caught my eye: Epson has come up with a specialized autofeeding duplex photo scanner (*FastFoto FF-680W*). One strongpoint of this device is that its duplex function is achieved not by flipping the paper over and re-scanning it but by implementing two independent sensors that can capture both sides in a single pass. This not only adds speed but more importantly reduces the risk of mechanical failure and damage associated with turning the paper.

Epson FastFoto FF-680W

With a device like this it is well possible to scan batches of photos (up to 36 at a time) and achieve a meaningfully efficient workflow.

In practice this specific device handles its main job of scanning photos quite well but leaves the user with very limited configuration options when it comes to naming files, organizing folders etc.

It is safe to say that if your photos are neatly stacked as they came out of the lab it will be easy prey for a device like this one. *I have even used it to capture the notes on back sides of photos even though I had those images already scanned from negatives.*

Glass Plates and Large Transparencies

These are very special and rare types of photographic media. If we have any of these in our possession chances are that lot of effort went into the production of these and that some meaningful value might be contained within.

Glass plates had been used in the early decades of photography as negatives from which prints were exposed by direct contact (*e.g. without any enlarging*). We can treat them like any other large format negatives (*with the extra care that their old age deserves*) and scan them on a transparency scanner like the Epson 700..850.

Similarly large format flexible sheet negatives have been used in professional photography and we can handle them the same way.

To be even more professional we can use a technique called fluid mounting (*or wet mounting, wet scanning etc.*): This puts a layer of special liquid between the glass of the scanner and the negative to eliminate possible interference caused by the air pockets in between these two surfaces.

3D Photos

We have two eyes and the ability of stereoscopic 3D vision – and once in a while photography and/or cinematography tries to take advantage of that ability before it rolls back to the 2D ordinary. Over the decades there have been several periods of increased interest in 3D photography and cinema- The last such surge took place around 2010 through approximately 2015 with major industry players producing 3D TVs, cameras, picture frames, even mobile phones.

Earlier many have experimented with 3D photography and left behind a variety of physical formats carrying pairs of left/right eye photographs. If we set out to digitize these rare treasures we simply need to find a way to scan/photograph each of the images under conditions as similar as possible with each other.

Then when we get the stereoscopic pair we can just save it for the future being marked L and R and hope that someone will find a way of viewing them – or we can go a step farther and combine both images into a single (usually MPO) file. For that purpose we can use a tool like the excellent "Stereo Photo Maker" that can be downloaded for free.

Among the rare physical formats of 3D pictures arguably the least rare might be the venerable:

ViewMaster Reels

This invention went big around the world in the 1960's. It is basically a round cardboard reel containing 7 pairs of evenly spaced image windows of about 10*12mm. These reels were mass produced as a medium to carry slideshows of tourist destinations, shows and movies, celebrities and just anything even including some erotica.

Apart from mass production thee were also cameras and production sets that enabled the individual shooting and framing of this wonderful form on standard 16mm or 35mm film.

Since these do carry some wonderful memories (and they do decay like all analog film does) it makes sense to digitize them for posterity.

The basic scanning is not too challenging: Excellent results can be obtained by just placing the reels on the glass surface of a good transparency scanner (at least 2000 DPI is a must).

The challenging part comes with correctly aligning and separating the image pairs which tends to be a tedious and demanding process requiring some DIY creativity.

Since I have developed an efficient workflow for this I take the liberty to offer my commercial digitization service if you need to transform some of these 3D treasures.

All things considered: I believe that people will continue using 2 eyes and a stereoscopic vision so it makes sense to preserve stereoscopic images in spite of the fact that currently there are only limited ways of viewing them.

74

Digitizing Videos

A few years ago it used to be easy to digitize VHS (and similar) video media by connecting the home video player to the input of a digital recorder or a special (a.k.a. Frame Grabber) computer input. Nowadays the cassettes are degrading in quality, VHS players are scarce and unreliable so it is becoming more and more common to opt for a professional video conversion service.

Emergency: Digitize Magnetic Tapes Now

Before you read on please beware: If you have any valuable content on analog video or audio tapes or similar, do not waste any time before converting these to a digital form. This is because the quality of these media degrades over time and the sooner you rescue them from their analog degradation the better.

DIY

If you still have a working device that can play your videos (VHS, SVHS, Hi-8, Betamax... etc...) you are well started to do your digitization yourself because the other tools you will need are quite simple and inexpensive.

First of all you will need some kind of adapter that will convert the (analog) output of your video to a (usually USB) input of your computer. There are many inexpensive devices on the market looking approximately like this:

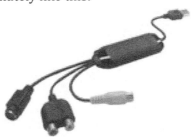

Be sure to check whether the device comes with the correct drivers (pieces of software) to work with your computer's operating system e.g. Windows 10. Also it is wise to check the type of USB supported. The usual standard is USB 2.0 which is OK. I would not recommendg going down to USB 1 while a USB 3.x would be an advantage though a minor one.

You may also need an adapter for connecting to SCART outputs (the antique connectors shaped like a distorted rectangle] like this one:

Then with the video streaming into the inside of the computer we will need some software to capture it. We can very well do with free programs like the

VirtualDub

which will capture the video content and store it is MPEG-2 (DVD) format and

HandBrake

which can transform your videos into the better MPEG-4 format.

My Favorite

There are many ways of editing videos most of which include a Video Editor software. These are indispensable for creative purposes, however for the purpose of archiving there may be other simpler ways:

For years I have been doing some video operations using a Panasonic DVD/Bluray recorder e.g. the venerable DMR-EX88. It hosts the possibility of simple no-fuss editing on the TV screen without the need for final rendering (export which may take a long time). The output from the recorder was to a DVD disk. That DVD I would keep as an archival disk and/or rip it to get the video files into my computer.

However the previous applies only to the older versions of Panasonic recorders (pre – 2018) which still had an analog input. So the newer ones have no way of accepting the wired signal from our old videos . However the new ones offer the wonderful possibility to transfer the resulting videos directly to your computer using a software like the **MediaMonkey** *so I might still continue using this in some variation of my workflow .*

Broken VHS Cassettes

The video cassettes are mechanical devices which can break or become jammed for some reason that did not destroy the information recorded therein. Much too often valuable videos have been thrown out after the first failed attempt to play them even though their contents could have been rescued.

Please be aware that very often a video cassette can be repaired – at least to the extent that it can be played once and digitized. You can try it DIY with the help of numerous how-tos on the web (do read the instructions please) or you can just ask the company that offers professional video digitization.

Rule of thumb: *As long as most of the tape inside the cassette is undamaged there still is hope.*

Providing that we have somehow managed to convert our videos to a digital form we can move on to the next step in making them archivable:

Segmenting & Describing

Analog videos often have the disadvantage that they come on cassettes as a continuous stream not segmented by time or event recorded. Often the only objective clue is date/time recorded over the picture - that is if we are lucky and the camera operator left this ugly feature turned on. In order to make these treasures attractive for their future viewers we should try to improve this situation by finding out more about the videos and incorporating that information into our archive..

Tips

- Before editing/splitting your video file be sure to have a backup copy stored away to revert to in case something goes wrong during the editing.

- More advanced video media like the MiniDV cassettes avoid this problem by storing each take as a separate quasi-file with date digitally recorded.

The goal will be to split the digitized recordings into distinct pieces which we can date and describe. The ways to achieve this are not exactly simple.

There are free programs available for just this task. They can be found by googling "video splitter" but I have not yet found any one worth recommending.

One reasonable way if possible with Pinnacle or other video editors: When importing a video file the software tries to divide it into "takes" based on its own intelligence. We can then recombine the takes into segments of related content.

Apart from the previous disadvantage we can find an advantage similar to *"Advantage of the Roll"* on page 70 - content found on one cassette is likely to have something in common - a date or a subject.

Many of the previous thoughts will apply to the following section about another even older analog video format:

Personal Movies

Digitizing 8mm or 16mm is mostly the realm of professional services. A real movie scanner can be bought in the price range of 20k+ EUR and that would not make sense for any work smaller than 1000 reels. Also note that many providers offer to scan to full HD (1080 lines) resolution which may or may not be useful as the real content of the film is seldom better than PAL/NTSC (625/525 lines). Certainly if the intention is just to watch the output there is little added value in scanning to a resolution higher than the grain of the film. However if post-processing and digital improvement is intended then the added resolution is an advantage. This is true for all flavors of 8mm movies and most 16mm as well.

However a decent dynamic range (Dmax of 3.5 or more) is important for all film scanning.

Currently there are some inexpensive film scanners on the market. When compared with commercial digitization services they will give you some more creative freedom and consume a lot of your time and effort in the process.

BTW: If you do opt for the DIY approach be sure to be adequately prepared with things like splicing equipment and extra reels.

Creativity with 8mm movies

It is worth mentioning one neglected aspect of the 8mm movie technology that has to do with the field of view. As we can see in the picture the standard 8mm format uses the surface area of the film in a rather wasteful, inefficient, way:

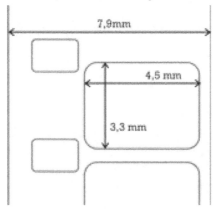

It can be seen that less than 50% of the area is used for its raison d'etre - for storing images. However some (or even most) camera makers did not feel the need to limit themselves to the designated picture area and allowed their cameras to expose a wider film area around the standardized frame. (I do not blame them as the real estate of the film was there so why not use it?)

Following is a real movie image from a real (Admira brand) camera from the 1960's :

We can see that there is a lot more on the film than in the standard (dotted) window. This may lead us to digitize more area than the standard would prescribe.

Like in the following image:

The videographer has concentrated on the lady in front and framed her correctly. However we might be also interested in the two people in the background.

We might even want to frame the image quite differently. Maybe like this:

In this case we even abandoned the original 4:3 aspect ratio and went for the contemporary 16:9 option. And moreover we admitted a part of perforation holes on the left – there is no shame in that – though we might as well decide against it.

Or you might encounter a different exposure shape like this product of a zoom lens on its wide end:

In fact I have even met (the output of) a camera with a really weird picture frame: Note the semicircular protrusion in the top right corner. I cannot find a reasonable explanation of what inside the camera mechanism could cause such an abberation :-)

Nevertheless in our preservation effort we might want to preserve even such an accidental fragment of a picture.

So such are some of the added degrees of freedom in DIY movie digitization.

Digitizing Audio

If we have any significant audio recordings they will probably come in the form of analog audio cassettes or – more scarcely – mini cartridges, reel to reel tapes or even phonograph records. Since the inherent quality of these media is far lesser than what we are used to in the digital environment it is usually

Audio cassettes

sufficient to digitize them by connecting the appropriate player to an audio input in our computer and make a recording using some software maybe as simple as the "Sound Recorder" included free with Windows under the "Accessories" tab in the start menu.

That is if we have access to the appropriate player. If not we might use a specialized digitization service. The catch here is that if our cassettes have not been marked with exceptional care we might be paying for the digitization of something random and worthless.

There are specialty consumer devices on the market (usually connecting via USB to your computer) for just this purpose. These can be used but will not add any real advantage to the process.

Digitizing Documents

We may have some very important documents worthy of being stored in our digital collection. These may include various certificates, diaries, passports, immigration forms etc.

It is rather easy to digitize these using any desktop scanner or a camera or even a smartphone. Just remember to

- store these in a future-proof format like JPG or PDF/A and

- equip them with a description and/or metadata

Digitizing the Digital

When dealing with antique digital media like floppy disks (a.k.a diskettes) or early vulnerable CD-ROMs we need to copy their contents to safe storage and apply most of the principles described in this book . This is not really digitization because the content already was digital but what needs to be done is very similar.

One important difference is that with old digital materials the Babel environment of early digital formats kicks in (see chapter "Obsolete Format" p. 17) Here we do not have the luxury of storing (the analog content) in the safest digital format possible and have to find a way of keeping the old content usable.

In any case the first rule is never to modify the original media. Any changes or conversions should be done on a separate copy.

If difficulties are encountered when reading these old media do not surrender yet: Often help is available through using special Data Recovery software of submitting to a professional service.

Diskettes

When trying to read old diskettes the operating system may encounter errors and (since it does not know how precious the ancient content is) prompt you to format (e.g. erase) the diskette like this:

NEVER comply with this request as it would decrease your chance of success at recovering the contents.

To further prevent any accidental erasure it is prudent to activate the write-protect switch or notch that is present on all diskettes.

CD-ROMs etc.

All CD based media (CD, DVD etc.) contain some form of error protection which makes them somewhat resilient to damage and deterioration. So if the CD manifests itself as readable it is best to copy its contents in 2 ways :

- as an ISO file (exact image of the disc)

- as files on the disc

If errors take place during reading there are lots of correction apps and professional services available to help.. Just google "Data Recovery"

Fostering Creation

In the process of organizing and capturing our digital heritage it may often hit us that we miss some kind of content simply because it was not yet created. This may be the simple requirement for photos of a certain place or object. Or it may invoke a more complicated task like having an old person write their memoirs or having them captured on video.

Write your Biography

It used to be a custom to write a diary and/or a biography at some stages of one's life. These have proven to be excellent integrating information sources for the future. By integrating I mean that a lot of meaningful information is stored there which may point to other documents and put them all in their context. In the past these personal recollections were done strictly as text while nowadays there is a strong urge to use audio or video recordings. I would urge to be conservative and resort to written text as much as possible because of its simple structure, comprehensiveness and self-organizing ability.

Record your Environment

It makes sense to record a video of things you consider important in your life. Unlike the integrating biography this can and should concentrate on a narrow topic, like maybe "My favorite tools" or "My bookcase","My neighborhood etc." The idea here is to capture things that are obvious now but will disappear in the future. I often wonder at how quick and intensive the process of disappearing tends to be.

> *Example:*
>
> *Sometimes I include the recordings from my car dashcam in my archive to help show the changes in the places that I drive through.*

Be Future-proof

Technology is evolving maybe too quickly. Over the last decades we see drastic improvements in features and quality of all things electronic as well as decreasing prices corresponding to various spinoffs of the famous Moore's law.

Therefore we can reasonably expect that even soon in the future people will be used to and be able to process much better digital data than we are today. The conclusion is to record our present in the best quality reasonably available. For instance in videos we should now (2019) not be content with anything below Full-HD (1,920x1,080) and rather opt for 4K (3,840x2,160 pixels).

Salvaging through Digitization

There are special cases when digitization is the only way of saving certain artifacts. One famous example are many books from the 19th century whose material -acid based paper- deteriorates so much that scanning them is the only way of salvaging their contents. We may not encounter such poignant situations in our lives but still we may face situations when a digital copy is all that is left of a physical object. Like when a photo gets lost/stolen and we are happy to at least have its digital image. Let us take such possibilities into account.

Storing Original Material

So we have scanned our photos, digitized the family movies etc. The question now is what to do with the original media. Chances are that no one will ever need to touch them especially now when their faithful copies are available through our computers, However there is a slight chance that a small portion of the original material will still be needed maybe for a scan of increased quality or to put on display etc. For such rare case we might still want to store the originals.

As we have mentioned earlier (on page 63) the most important thing is to have the material marked to prevent duplicate digitization. The next most important need is to **organize the material so that a specific piece can be found based on its digitized image.**

For this archival storage I often use ring binders with all sorts of matching document sleeves and pouches.

The digital preservationists use a funny abbreviation: LOCKSS which means: *Lots of Copies Keeps Stuff Safe*.

That is a deep and exact truth. In this context it means that if we make multiple copies of our archive and spread them around chances are that some of the copies will get found sometime.

In this chapter I would like to explore the possibilities of placing various forms of your information around the world - both physical and digital.

Online Copies

Digital material has the immense advantage of unlimited copying. If we have some material that we deem to be interesting for someone in the future let us try to insert it into as many interesting places as possible in the hope that someone will find and appreciate it.

Wikipedia

If there is one website that has the best chance of being preserved long into the future it is Wikipedia and/or one of its sister projects. Therefore having your content inserted into Wikipedia gives a lot of preservation value. However Wikipedians are quite picky about the content they admit - they have guidelines to select only content of public importance so it will take some effort to get inside.

And there is another catch: For any content to be accepted to any Wiki project its copyright has to be released to the public domain - therefore surrendering almost all your claims regarding the content. This may well be your intention with future-aiming content but may bring difficulty in some cases.

The admission policies however vary across various Wiki projects as follows:

Wikimedia Commons

This is basically a language-independent collection of photos and other audiovisual content. The admission to this collection is very liberal. Actually I have never seen them reject a photo except for cases of copyright violation. The photos are uploaded online and may be equipped with a rich collection of metadata including location, descriptions etc. The descriptions (*possibly in multiple languages*) are your chance for including links and clues leading to your other content.

If you are shy about releasing your photos to the public domain you still can

- release only a showpiece of a collection and refer to the whole collection in description
- release only a lower resolution of a photo

BTW: As I have written in a prior chapter on Metadata (p. 27): Uploading a photo to Wikimedia Commons is a great beginners' exercise in handling digitized content and its metadata.

WikiSources

This is mainly a collection of contents of books that have already been published. Sometimes it is possible to insert a self/published book but generally the Wikipedians are cautious about people pushing their own content and they usually require some proof of importance.

Wikipedia (the encyclopedia)

Wikipedia - the encyclopedia is heavily guarded against any biases or subjective material.

When it comes to starting a new topic - like a person's page - it must be proved that the person or topic is important enough.

When inserting information into an existing topic one must provide sources to back that information; otherwise deletes are quick and merciless. Wikipedia is so obsessed by sources that it usually allows the adding of links and references as long as they are relevant to the topic at least remotely. That way it is possible to insert some clues that may eventually lead a future reader to your content.

Anyone can edit Wikipedia but it is not very easy to understand the rules, customs and best practices. However there are always enough experienced wikipedians to push you around and teach until you do things to their liking.

A typical use-case is a bio page about one of your ancestors which will be allowed if you can provide some proof of their importance.

Websites and Online Archives

It is very easy to set up your own website around any topic or collection of materials. The site will work as long as some owner keeps their computers running and operating. If it is someone like Google that may be a long time indeed. And with a service like sites.google.com you can get the site for free. So anyone will be able to see your material for a long time on the order of decades.

To extend that longevity is the goal of web archiving projects spearheaded by web.archive.org. Its founder Brewster Kahle has set out to capture timestamped copies of the web to keep a worldwide historical record. Many others have followed like national libraries who collect their respective parts of the web. International coordination is done by the International Internet Preservation Consortium founded in close connection with the U.S. Library of Congress.

You can have your specific website harvested and included in those collections by writing directly to the digital librarians or indirectly by searching for your web address in those collections - that can let them know that your site exists and prompt them to harvest and store your site.

If you have a specific collection of recognizable historical value you might even get in touch with Archive.org (the Internet Archive) directly to have your collection included in their curated preservation efforts.

These archives are another way to have your content included in collections which are managed professionally and therefore have a huge chance of surviving long into the future.

Just make sure that your website is clean HTML and if possible avoid any scripting that might confuse the archiving machinery.

Genealogy Databases

There are a number of genealogy websites that are eager to accept your information regarding your family and your life. You can use that opportunity to include clues and links for finding the content you are trying to preserve or even parts of the content itself.

My personal favorite where I tend to store my family information is the rodovid.org which is shaped according to Wiki paradigms and quite stable.

After Your Physical Death

The task of preserving your digital heritage is not limited to your physical lifetime. While you are still active you do whatever you can. However after your demise you may want to hand over some instructions or information related -not only to- preserving your digital heritage. Actually Google has a service and process in place for this. It is called the Inactive Account Manager {https://myaccount.google.com/inactive } and it does exactly that: When you have not accessed your account for some time they make sure you are not responding and then hand over access to people of your choosing. This can well be used to let people know what to do about things that mattered to you.

These post-mortem instructions can very well point to a copy of your working archive along with instructions on what to do with it. And yes, feel free to pass on a copy of this book to help with the instructions.

Facebook has also moved forward in this area. It enables a process to "memorialize" a person's account - basically turning it into an archive under the supervision of a person'a appointed Legacy Contact. That can help our purpose.

I have no clue as to whether Google and Facebook will outlive us but it seems wise to prepare for that possibility and use the options that they provide.

The list does not end here

There is plenty of room for creativity in finding online places for storing and distributing your digital content. It would be great to share inspiration and good ideas.

Physical copies

Alongside putting our precious content in places on the internet we should also seek opportunities to put physical copies at remarkable spots in the real world, especially places that carry some significance that is likely to continue in the future. Excellent places would be church towers (though compromised by brutal temperature changes), historical monuments, museums etc.

> BTW: The absolute victory goes to the one who manages to place their collection inside one of the Egyptian pyramids :-)

To make our message even more attractive it may be essential to produce physical artifacts (prints, books ets.) that will attract some attention of our target group. Specifically books command a lot of respect in most western cultures so anything that looks like a book will get some extra care and preservation.

PhotoBooks

When "advertising" to a small community like the family of your descendants it may be effective to produce a book of photos. Due to their attractive form these have more hope of avoiding the trash can than ordinary dull digital media e.g. DVDs. Photobooks have the tendency to rest on shelves for decades -and let us presume- even centuries.

Make no mistake: Prints on paper do not preserve the full richness of your digital information. They are more like bait to draw users toward you content. That content itself may be attached to the book by means of a disc inserted into the book. A good way is to secure the disc inside the book cover using a self-adhesive sleeve.

I would prefer to use a paper sleeve/envelope to mount the disk in the book. However if the sleeve is plastic I would insert a sheet of clear velum or similar quality paper as a separator between the active side of the DVD and the plastic pocket to prevent the two surfaces from sticking together.

This way when 100 years later someone browses the book they may be tempted to explore the additional content on the disc - and that is where we want to lead them.

Another less trustworthy way of pointing from a book toward digital content would be to print a web address or search parameters leading to your digital content online (in the form of text URL or a QR code like those used in this book) . The risk here is that the online world is likely to change quite dramatically so the links may not be valid for long.

Self-Published Books

Let us take the concept of a self-published photobook to another level: There are well established services that will take your content, print it into a book, assign it an ISBN (International Standard Book Number) an established identifier that tells the world that the book exists and has it included in all sorts of library databases. With an ISBN your book gets an extra measure of authority and becomes more findable.

All you need to do is format your content into a PDF file and upload it to the publisher. If you make the book for public sale you have just ascertained having it in online storage for possibly decades - where someone can notice it and order a copy. Or you can just order your own copies and distribute them (hopefully with inserted discs) to your local libraries and similar safe places. Very probably there are archives and/or libraries in your town or parish or university etc. that will be happy to accept your materials.

So far I do not know of any on-demand printing service that would offer to attach a disc in their production. If there is one please let me know.

From my own experience I can recommend CreateSpace (recently renamed Amazon Kindle Direct Publishing https://kdp.amazon.com/) which inserts your paperbacks and e-books directly and swiftly into Amazon's catalog for sale. Another excellent provider is Lulu www.lulu.com who allow paperbacks as well as hardcover books and provide a better print quality (e.g. for photos).

When your book has an ISBN it might even have a chance of being accepted to your national library (e.g. the U.S. Library of Congress) where it will enjoy a great level of physical preservation for centuries by library professionals. Currently the national libraries (led by for example the British Library) are starting to accept e-books (digital content itself) into their collections so we may soon be able to get a powerful protection for our digital files directly.

Global Heritage Deposits

Similar to large national libraries there are a number of preservation initiatives with the ambition of collecting important digital materials and preserve them. Once in a time some of these put a DVD on a space satellite or on the moon, in deep caves, on mountaintops, in bunkers etc. Some of these may be open to include your content - maybe for a fee.

Among these I would name the Arch Mission Foundation (www.archmission.org) which may do just that for you.

Framed Pictures

A well printed beautiful picture in a fancy frame is a great place on the back of which a digital archive disc can be stored. Even better if the topic of the picture has to do with the archive. Like a family portrait would fit well a family archive.

And similarly we can think of many creative ways where to put physical copies of archive to facilitate its preservation.

Make it Known

Last not least: Be sure that your family and/or neighborhood, friends, colleagues etc. know about your archive. These are the first people who will carry the word and perhaps cause your archive to be noticed by someone in the future.

Short Summary of What to Do

Recommended Actions

To those who want to quickly move to action or just capture the essence of what this book is about I would offer the following action points:

- Collect your digital valuables in one place on your desktop disk or archive server

- Digitize your valuable old assets

- Use standard simple file formats such as TXT, HTML, JPG, MP2, PDF/A

- Provide additional information to describe your valuable files

- Make copies of your archive on long-lasting (M-Disc or similar) disks

- Put those copies in findable places in the physical world and online

- Find ways how to let your descendants know that the archive exists and how to find it

These are the basic recommended actions. The inside of this book has tried to explain the previous steps in detail.

I have tried to provide a practice-oriented set of recipes for basic personal digital preservation. You may however delve deeper into the world of Digital Preservation which is inhabited by professional librarians and curators. The following references wil serve that purpose:

Owens, Trevor [2018-12-10T22:58:59]. The Theory and Craft of Digital Preservation . Johns Hopkins University Press.

This book gives an excellent overview from the perspective of a digital librarian. I would especially recommend meditating the author's set of „*Sixteen Guiding Digital Preservation Axioms*" from which I would quote:

- Nothing has been preserved, there are only things **being** preserved.

- Hoarding is not preservation.

- Backing up data is not digital preservation.

- The boundaries of digital objects are fuzzy.

Harvey, Ross [2018-03-01T22:58:59]. Preserving Digital Materials . Rowman & Littlefield Publishers.

This book provides a well thought-out systematic overview of why and what to preserve.

*The complete guide to personal digital archiving /
edited by Brianna H. Marshall. (2018-10-
27T23:58:59).   American Library Association.*

This is written from the standpoint of archiving science and
tends to be scientifically punctual and exhausting.

File: Digital_Immortality_1_95

Date: 2020-12-26